Yasmine Ben Salmi aka Lovepreneur

CAN I ASK YOU A QUESTION DOCTOR?

–

NEUROLOGY

Edition with Mr Chidiebere Ibe

Written by Award-Winning Author Yasmine Ben Salmi &
Illustrated by Chidiebere Ibe

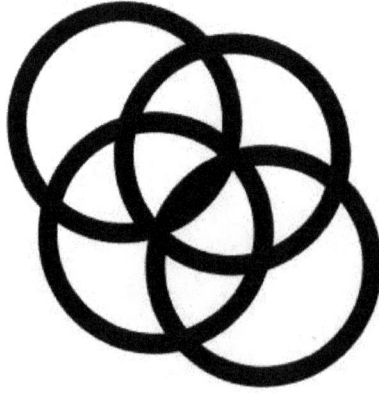

The Choice is Yours

PUBLISHING

DEDICATION

I dedicate this book to you, the reader because you are amazing.

CAN I ASK YOU A QUESTION DOCTOR?

ACKNOWLEDGMENTS

I would like to acknowledge my family, friends and each doctor who participated in this medical series. I would also like to take this moment to say a special thank you to Mr Chidiebere Ibe for answering my questions and for sharing his life journey with us in this book.

CAN I ASK YOU A QUESTION DOCTOR?

–

NEUROLOGY

Edition with Mr Chidiebere Ibe

Written by Award-Winning Author Yasmine Ben Salmi & Illustrated by Mr Chidiebere Ibe

Hi there, my name is Yasmine Ben Salmi aka Lovepreneur, and I am 14-years-old.
I dream of becoming an orthodontist or a plastic surgeon someday. Today I am going to explore the fascinating world of NEUROLOGY. Come explore the medical industry with me in this medical series where I get to ask a host of neurologists thought-provoking questions.

Hello Mr Ibe, can you please introduce yourself to our readers by telling them your name, profession and what you do for a living?

Mr Ibe responded:

"My name is Chidiebere Ibe. I am from Ebonyi State in Nigeria. I am a medical student majoring with major Neurology at the Kyiv Medical University, Ukraine. I got my first degree from the University of Uyo, Nigeria, where I studied Chemistry. I am an Afro skin medical illustrator".

GLIOMA

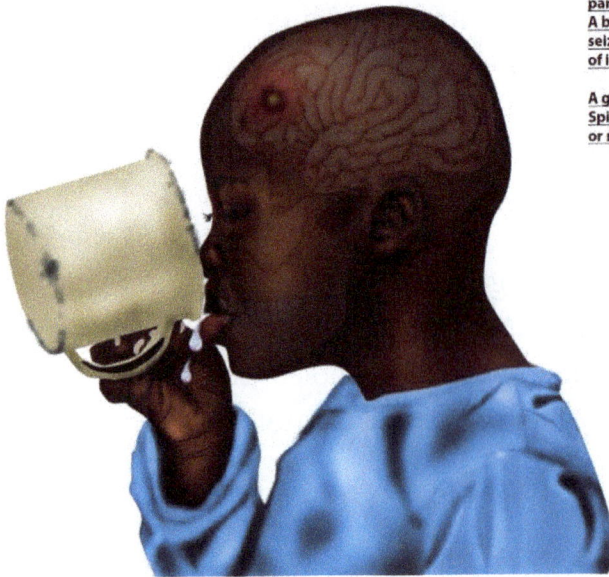

A glioma is a type of tumor that starts in the glial cells of the brain or the spine.

Symptoms of gliomas depend on which part of the central nervous system is affected. A brain glioma can cause headaches, vomiting, seizures, and cranial nerve disorders as a result of increased intracranial pressure.

A glioma of the optic nerve can cause visual loss. Spinal cord gliomas can cause pain, weakness, or numbness in the extremities.

Chidiebere Ibe
IG: ebereillustrate
Twitter: ebereillustrate

I am super excited about exploring neurology with you

Mr Ibe.

Mr Ibe responded: "Yes, I am equally very excited".

So, Chidiebere Ibe what inspired your initial interest in the medical industry and why did you become a doctor?

Mr Ibe responded:

"What initially inspired my interest was just the passion for medicine because when I was a child the first career, I ever choose was to be a medical doctor; I had never thought of any other career than to be in the medical industry. What propelled me more to keep on pursuing my dream was when I lost my mum to ovarian cancer. I was very young and that kept my drive alive to be in the health industry, to become a doctor and to be able to provide services and evict pain from people through surgery. That was what inspired my interest in being a doctor and going into the health sector."

Oh, wow that is an interesting perspective because when I was growing up, I didn't know much about your area of expertise.

Mr Ibe responded:

"Areas like neurology haven't really been talked about, medical students are rarely advised to go into areas of neurology (neurosurgery) because of the time frame to complete a residency, the time frame to become a full neurosurgeon. When I was growing up, I had never heard of areas pertaining to neurology; all I heard about was gynaecology, obstetrics and paediatrics. Areas of neurology were not mentioned."

I am intrigued to learn more about you and your story, please delve a little deeper?

Mr Ibe responded:

"I am a twenty-five-year-old Nigerian. I belong to a family of five. I have three wonderful siblings. I am a self-taught medical illustrator and at the point of this interview, it was one year and seven months in medical illustrations. I have a mentor who has always given me advice pertaining to my choice of career.
I grew up in a difficult background.

I tried medical school for five years and I was not admitted. It was sad and depressing but that led me to learn skills like photography, graphic design, videography and animation and putting all of this together has made me successful in my expertise today both in neurology and medical illustration, I am very grateful for it all."

What do you feel are the most rewarding aspects of being a doctor within your field?

Mr Ibe responded:

"You are able to be a contributing factor to the global health system. In Africa, there is a limited number of neurosurgeons and being in the area of neurology especially in Africa gives you the privilege to be an impact on Africa's healthcare system and of course I think that's a superior reward. I believe the most rewarding aspect is to impact society and being able to see people's pain and relate to their pain and be able to proffer solutions to their pains."

What do you feel is often misunderstood about becoming a doctor within the area of your expertise?

Mr Ibe responded:

"One of it is that you never fully become a neurosurgeon, that's cliché because there are a lot of neurosurgeons right now; it's just a concept that the years of training are very long and arduous, so people already suggest or conclude that being a neurosurgeon is typically not possible.

Another misunderstanding people have is that neurosurgeons only focus on the brain; no, that's not true, being a neurological surgeon also involves taking care of the human spines, and nervous system."

What have been some of your most memorable moments in your career both good and bad and how did these memorable moments shape you?

Mr Ibe responded:

"The most memorable moment in my life was trying to get into medical school and was not admitted. It was a difficult period for me. It made me depressed; it made me make comparisons to others; it made me think less of myself and I wasn't able to focus on the big picture which is trying again and trying harder.

That was the moment I met someone that changed my life, my mentor, Dr Sydney, he was able to groom me and made me become a better person through his advice and mentorship. He advised me that in careers like medicine, I had to make a decision to put my best into it and make the most out of it."

What do you now know that you wish you had known when you began your career as a doctor?

Mr Ibe responded:

"I wish I had known earlier that everything happens in the process because before medical school I was impatient, I wanted things to happen immediately. I didn't understand that everything works in process, and everything has its time and moment and I had to learn in the process of growing; I had to learn that in a very hard way. If I knew this earlier, I would never have forced things to happen."

What message and 3-10 tips would you give to your younger self?

Mr Ibe responded:

"The message I will give myself is a message of self-love. Growing up as a child, I had low self-esteem making comparisons based on my background wishing I had wealthier parents giving me everything I wanted in life. I failed to love and value myself.

The message I would give my younger self is to love myself irrespective of the background I come from. Tips I would give my younger self: Is to understand the process. Value the background I came from. Learn to develop my mind with. And learn to forgive myself for the things I did wrong. Have faith in the impossible."

Can you explain your career path from academic to practising?

Mr Ibe responded:

"My career path started from doing a pre-degree in chemistry
which was a difficult moment of my studies. I did chemistry because
I tried medical school for years and I wasn't admitted so from my first
degree in chemistry to applying to medical school and
eventually getting admitted into medical school and also being able
to combine my medical knowledge with my artistic skills which fall into
medical illustrations."

What are some of the things that young people should be aware of if they desire to become a doctor in their area of expertise?

Mr Ibe responded:

"Young people should be aware of things like the process involved in becoming a neurological surgeon, it's going to be a difficult process and young people should be aware of the price that they have to pay to become that because at some point in life the journey to becoming a neurological surgeon will make some persons fret: some people give up; some people fall out of purpose, desire, intention, some will forget the reasons why they wanted to be a neurological surgeon. So, one thing I would tell young people is that, they should be aware that it will become very difficult, and they may want to quit but they should remember why they started."

What were your dreams and aspirations when you were 14-years old?

Mr Ibe responded:

"Become a doctor!
Become a doctor!!
Become a doctor!!!"

What areas of your medical profession would you like to expand into?

Mr Ibe responded:

"Neurogenomics"

What challenges or setbacks have you had to overcome in order to
get to where you are today?

Mr Ibe responded:

"The greatest challenge I went through was the challenge of not
having my family's support because after my first degree in
chemistry I wanted to go back to being a medical doctor; my family
discouraged me and talked me out of it and said they weren't going to
sponsor me in schools. It was a challenge for me so I decided to learn a
lot of skills that will generate resources for me to pay my
tuition, so I deliberately learnt skills like photography and graphic design
to raise tuition."

How do you deal with your stress levels from such a demanding career?

Mr Ibe responded:

"Personally, I work better under stress and generally how I deal with stress is that whenever I get inundated with so many tasks, I simply write them down and unconsciously I feel like I have achieved those goals already. What I do next is to deal with the most difficult task first before the easier tasks and when I do that it reduces my stress level.

So basically, careers that are demanding and overwhelming like neurology, it is important to prioritise activities in order to manage and deal with your stress level."

What are three key principles that I must learn to help me in my journey?

Mr Ibe responded:

"First, the principle of time management because everything happens in the space of time. Another principle is the principle of hard work and smart work because most successful people are known for working hard and not just working hard but also working smart.To be in a medical field, you have to be able to think smart to apply smart techniques at a required time. The principle of self-improvement because you cannot give what you do not have, and you cannot become your ultimate self without giving yourself value."

How will I know if I am on the right track?

Mr Ibe responded:

"You will always know that you are on the right track because there's this instinct that is always telling us that we are doing it right or wrong, or we are doing the right things that will lead us to the right path or the right destination. The issue with being on the right path, is that people lie to themselves a lot just to suit their interest but if people don't focus full attention on themselves, they will not know if they are on the right track or not.

And also, one of the good signs that show you are on the right track is you always have doors of opportunities open for you, you always have people coming to help you, people coming to your aid most of the time and that's a sign you are on the right track. Another sign is that most time it gets very difficult, because if we are destined to do a task, life circumstances bring challenges our way to build us in that track and that's why we shouldn't give up on that track."

Thank you so much for answering all my questions, do you have a final message that you would like to share?

Mr Ibe responded:

"My final message is to keep faith alive, believe and have faith in every possibility that you can exude. Thank you."

I hope that you enjoyed my conversation with this doctor. Be sure to look out for the other five doctors in this series

"CAN I ASK YOU A QUESTION DOCTOR? – NEUROLOGY"

A SPECIAL QUOTE FROM YASMINE

"Love is not a destination; it is a state of BEING - so be gentle with
yourself and others around you."
Yasmine Ben Salmi aka Lovepreneur

DAILY REFLECTION JOURNAL

Writing things down is an effective way of remembering and reflecting on all the amazing things that happen every day.

No matter how much you write or how little you write, take the time to really think about your day, at the end of your journal you can then go back and treasure those memories.

Date: __/__/____ Today I am Grateful For...

_____

_____

_____

_____

What Would Make Today A Great Day?

_____

_____

During the evening just before going to bed take a moment to reflect on your day then List the 3 best things that happened…

1) _____

_____

2) _____

_____

3) _____

_____

Date: __/__/____ Today I am Grateful For...

_____

_____

_____

_____

What Would Make Today A Great Day?

_____

_____

During the evening just before going to bed take a moment to reflect on your day then List

the 3 best things that happened...

1) _____

_____

2) _____

_____

3) _____

_____

Date: __/__/____ Today I am Grateful For…

_____

_____

_____

_____

What Would Make Today A Great Day?

_____

_____

During the evening just before going to bed take a moment to reflect on your day then List the 3 best things that happened…

1) _____

_____

2) _____

_____

3) _____

_____

Date: __/__/____ Today I am Grateful For…

_____

_____

_____

_____

What Would Make Today A Great Day?

_____

_____

During the evening just before going to bed take a moment to reflect on your day then List the 3 best things that happened…

1) _____

_____

2) _____

_____

3) _____

_____

Date: __/__/____ Today I am Grateful For...

_____

_____

_____

_____

What Would Make Today A Great Day?

_____

_____

During the evening just before going to bed take a moment to reflect on your day then List the 3 best things that happened...

1) _____

_____

2) _____

_____

3) _____

_____

Date: __/__/____ Today I am Grateful For...

_____

_____

_____

_____

What Would Make Today A Great Day?

_____

_____

During the evening just before going to bed take a moment to reflect on your day then List the 3 best things that happened...

1) _____

_____

2) _____

_____

3) _____

_____

Date: __/__/____ Today I am Grateful For...

_____

_____

_____

_____

What Would Make Today A Great Day?

_____

_____

During the evening just before going to bed take a moment to reflect on your day then List the 3 best things that happened...

1) _____

_____

2) _____

_____

3) _____

_____

Date: __/__/____ Today I am Grateful For...

_____

_____

_____

_____

What Would Make Today A Great Day?

_____

_____

During the evening just before going to bed take a moment to reflect on your day then List

the 3 best things that happened...

1) _____

_____

2) _____

_____

3) _____

_____

Date: __/__/____ Today I am Grateful For...

_____

_____

_____

_____

What Would Make Today A Great Day?

_____

_____

During the evening just before going to bed take a moment to reflect on your day then List the 3 best things that happened...

1) _____

_____

2) _____

_____

3) _____

_____

Date: __/__/____ Today I am Grateful For...

_____

_____

_____

_____

What Would Make Today A Great Day?

_____

_____

During the evening just before going to bed take a moment to reflect on your day then List

the 3 best things that happened...

1) _____

_____

2) _____

_____

3) _____

_____

Date: __/__/____ Today I am Grateful For…

_____

_____

_____

_____

What Would Make Today A Great Day?

_____

_____

During the evening just before going to bed take a moment to reflect on your day then List the 3 best things that happened…

1) _____

_____

2) _____

_____

3) _____

_____

Date: __/__/____ Today I am Grateful For…

_____

_____

_____

_____

What Would Make Today A Great Day?

_____

_____

During the evening just before going to bed take a moment to reflect on your day then List the 3 best things that happened…

1) _____

_____

2) _____

_____

3) _____

_____

Date: __/__/____ Today I am Grateful For...

_____

_____

_____

_____

What Would Make Today A Great Day?

_____

_____

During the evening just before going to bed take a moment to reflect on your day then List the 3 best things that happened...

1) _____

_____

2) _____

_____

3) _____

_____

Date: __/__/____ Today I am Grateful For…

_____

_____

_____

_____

What Would Make Today A Great Day?

_____

_____

During the evening just before going to bed take a moment to reflect on your day then List the 3 best things that happened…

1) _____

_____

2) _____

_____

3) _____

_____

Date: __/__/____ Today I am Grateful For...

_____

_____

_____

_____

What Would Make Today A Great Day?

_____

_____

During the evening just before going to bed take a moment to reflect on your day then List the 3 best things that happened...

1) _____

_____

2) _____

_____

3) _____

_____

Date: __/__/____ Today I am Grateful For…

_____

_____

_____

_____

What Would Make Today A Great Day?

_____

_____

During the evening just before going to bed take a moment to reflect on your day then List the 3 best things that happened…

1) _____

_____

2) _____

_____

3) _____

_____

Date: __/__/____ Today I am Grateful For...

_____

_____

_____

_____

What Would Make Today A Great Day?

_____

_____

During the evening just before going to bed take a moment to reflect on your day then List the 3 best things that happened...

1) _____

_____

2) _____

_____

3) _____

_____

Date: __/__/____ Today I am Grateful For...

_____

_____

_____

_____

What Would Make Today A Great Day?

_____

_____

During the evening just before going to bed take a moment to reflect on your day then List

the 3 best things that happened...

1) _____

_____

2) _____

_____

3) _____

_____

Date: __/__/____ Today I am Grateful For...

_____

_____

_____

_____

What Would Make Today A Great Day?

_____

_____

During the evening just before going to bed take a moment to reflect on your day then List the 3 best things that happened...

1) _____

_____

2) _____

_____

3) _____

_____

Date: __/__/____ Today I am Grateful For...

_____

_____

_____

_____

What Would Make Today A Great Day?

_____

_____

During the evening just before going to bed take a moment to reflect on your day then List the 3 best things that happened...

1) _____

_____

2) _____

_____

3) _____

_____

Date: __/__/____ Today I am Grateful For…

_____

_____

_____

_____

What Would Make Today A Great Day?

_____

_____

During the evening just before going to bed take a moment to reflect on your day then List the 3 best things that happened…

1) _____

_____

2) _____

_____

3) _____

_____

Date: __/__/____ Today I am Grateful For...

_____

_____

_____

_____

What Would Make Today A Great Day?

_____

_____

During the evening just before going to bed take a moment to reflect on your day then List

the 3 best things that happened...

1) _____

_____

2) _____

_____

3) _____

_____

Date: __/__/____ Today I am Grateful For...

_____

_____

_____

_____

What Would Make Today A Great Day?

_____

_____

During the evening just before going to bed take a moment to reflect on your day then List the 3 best things that happened...

1) _____

_____

2) _____

_____

3) _____

_____

Date: __/__/____ Today I am Grateful For…

_____

_____

_____

_____

What Would Make Today A Great Day?

_____

_____

During the evening just before going to bed take a moment to reflect on your day then List the 3 best things that happened…

1) _____

_____

2) _____

_____

3) _____

_____

Date: __/__/____ Today I am Grateful For...

_____

_____

_____

_____

What Would Make Today A Great Day?

_____

_____

During the evening just before going to bed take a moment to reflect on your day then List the 3 best things that happened...

1) _____

_____

2) _____

_____

3) _____

_____

Date: __/__/____ Today I am Grateful For...

_____

_____

_____

_____

What Would Make Today A Great Day?

_____

_____

During the evening just before going to bed take a moment to reflect on your day then List the 3 best things that happened...

1) _____

_____

2) _____

_____

3) _____

_____

Date: __/__/____ Today I am Grateful For...

_____

_____

_____

_____

What Would Make Today A Great Day?

_____

_____

During the evening just before going to bed take a moment to reflect on your day then List the 3 best things that happened...

1) _____

_____

2) _____

_____

3) _____

_____

Date: __/__/____ Today I am Grateful For…

_____

_____

_____

_____

What Would Make Today A Great Day?

_____

_____

During the evening just before going to bed take a moment to reflect on your day then List

the 3 best things that happened…

1) _____

_____

2) _____

_____

3) _____

_____

Date: __/__/____ Today I am Grateful For...

_____

_____

_____

_____

What Would Make Today A Great Day?

_____

_____

During the evening just before going to bed take a moment to reflect on your day then List the 3 best things that happened...

1) _____

_____

2) _____

_____

3) _____

_____

Date: __/__/____ Today I am Grateful For...

_____

_____

_____

_____

What Would Make Today A Great Day?

_____

_____

During the evening just before going to bed take a moment to reflect on your day then List

the 3 best things that happened...

1) _____

_____

2) _____

_____

3) _____

_____

Date: __/__/____ Today I am Grateful For...

_____

_____

_____

_____

What Would Make Today A Great Day?

_____

_____

During the evening just before going to bed take a moment to reflect on your day then List the 3 best things that happened...

1) _____

_____

2) _____

_____

3) _____

_____

Date: __/__/____ Today I am Grateful For…

_____

_____

_____

_____

What Would Make Today A Great Day?

_____

_____

During the evening just before going to bed take a moment to reflect on your day then List the 3 best things that happened…

1) _____

_____

2) _____

_____

3) _____

_____

Date: __/__/____ Today I am Grateful For…

_____

_____

_____

_____

What Would Make Today A Great Day?

_____

_____

During the evening just before going to bed take a moment to reflect on your day then List the 3 best things that happened…

1) _____

_____

2) _____

_____

3) _____

_____

Date: __/__/____ Today I am Grateful For…

_____

_____

_____

_____

What Would Make Today A Great Day?

_____

_____

During the evening just before going to bed take a moment to reflect on your day then List

the 3 best things that happened…

1) _____

_____

2) _____

_____

3) _____

_____

Date: __/__/____ Today I am Grateful For...

_____

_____

_____

_____

What Would Make Today A Great Day?

_____

_____

During the evening just before going to bed take a moment to reflect on your day then List the 3 best things that happened...

1) _____

_____

2) _____

_____

3) _____

_____

Date: __/__/____ Today I am Grateful For...

_____

_____

_____

_____

What Would Make Today A Great Day?

_____

_____

During the evening just before going to bed take a moment to reflect on your day then List the 3 best things that happened...

1) _____

_____

2) _____

_____

3) _____

_____

Date: __/__/____ Today I am Grateful For...

_____

_____

_____

_____

What Would Make Today A Great Day?

_____

_____

During the evening just before going to bed take a moment to reflect on your day then List the 3 best things that happened...

1) _____

_____

2) _____

_____

3) _____

_____

Date: __/__/____ Today I am Grateful For...

_____

_____

_____

_____

What Would Make Today A Great Day?

_____

_____

During the evening just before going to bed take a moment to reflect on your day then List

the 3 best things that happened...

1) _____

_____

2) _____

_____

3) _____

_____

Date: __/__/____ Today I am Grateful For...

_____

_____

_____

_____

What Would Make Today A Great Day?

_____

_____

During the evening just before going to bed take a moment to reflect on your day then List the 3 best things that happened...

1) _____

_____

2) _____

_____

3) _____

_____

Date: __/__/____ Today I am Grateful For...

_____

_____

_____

_____

What Would Make Today A Great Day?

_____

_____

During the evening just before going to bed take a moment to reflect on your day then List

the 3 best things that happened...

1) _____

_____

2) _____

_____

3) _____

_____

Date: __/__/____ Today I am Grateful For...

_____

_____

_____

_____

What Would Make Today A Great Day?

_____

_____

During the evening just before going to bed take a moment to reflect on your day then List the 3 best things that happened...

1) _____

_____

2) _____

_____

3) _____

_____

Date: __/__/____ Today I am Grateful For…

_____

_____

_____

_____

What Would Make Today A Great Day?

_____

_____

During the evening just before going to bed take a moment to reflect on your day then List

the 3 best things that happened…

1) _____

_____

2) _____

_____

3) _____

_____

Date: __/__/____ Today I am Grateful For…

_____

_____

_____

_____

What Would Make Today A Great Day?

_____

_____

During the evening just before going to bed take a moment to reflect on your day then List

the 3 best things that happened…

1) _____

_____

2) _____

_____

3) _____

_____

Date: __/__/____ Today I am Grateful For...

_____

_____

_____

_____

What Would Make Today A Great Day?

_____

_____

During the evening just before going to bed take a moment to reflect on your day then List the 3 best things that happened...

1) _____

_____

2) _____

_____

3) _____

_____

Date: __/__/____ Today I am Grateful For…

_____

_____

_____

_____

What Would Make Today A Great Day?

_____

_____

During the evening just before going to bed take a moment to reflect on your day then List the 3 best things that happened…

1) _____

_____

2) _____

_____

3) _____

_____

Date: __/__/____ Today I am Grateful For…

_____

_____

_____

_____

What Would Make Today A Great Day?

_____

_____

During the evening just before going to bed take a moment to reflect on your day then List

the 3 best things that happened…

1) _____

_____

2) _____

_____

3) _____

_____

Date: __/__/____ Today I am Grateful For...

_____

_____

_____

_____

What Would Make Today A Great Day?

_____

_____

During the evening just before going to bed take a moment to reflect on your day then List the 3 best things that happened...

1) _____

_____

2) _____

_____

3) _____

_____

Date: __/__/____ Today I am Grateful For...

_____

_____

_____

_____

What Would Make Today A Great Day?

_____

_____

During the evening just before going to bed take a moment to reflect on your day then List the 3 best things that happened...

1) _____

_____

2) _____

_____

3) _____

_____

Date: __/__/____ Today I am Grateful For...

_____

_____

_____

_____

What Would Make Today A Great Day?

_____

_____

During the evening just before going to bed take a moment to reflect on your day then List the 3 best things that happened...

1) _____

_____

2) _____

_____

3) _____

_____

Date: __/__/____ Today I am Grateful For...

_____

_____

_____

_____

What Would Make Today A Great Day?

_____

_____

During the evening just before going to bed take a moment to reflect on your day then List the 3 best things that happened...

1) _____

_____

2) _____

_____

3) _____

_____

Date: __/__/____ Today I am Grateful For...

_____

_____

_____

_____

What Would Make Today A Great Day?

_____

_____

During the evening just before going to bed take a moment to reflect on your day then List

the 3 best things that happened...

1) _____

_____

2) _____

_____

3) _____

_____

Date: __/__/____ Today I am Grateful For...

_____

_____

_____

_____

What Would Make Today A Great Day?

_____

_____

During the evening just before going to bed take a moment to reflect on your day then List the 3 best things that happened...

1) _____

_____

2) _____

_____

3) _____

_____

Date: __/__/____ Today I am Grateful For…

_____

_____

_____

_____

What Would Make Today A Great Day?

_____

_____

During the evening just before going to bed take a moment to reflect on your day then List the 3 best things that happened…

1) _____

_____

2) _____

_____

3) _____

_____

Date: __/__/____ Today I am Grateful For…

_____

_____

_____

_____

What Would Make Today A Great Day?

_____

_____

During the evening just before going to bed take a moment to reflect on your day then List

the 3 best things that happened…

1) _____

_____

2) _____

_____

3) _____

_____

Date: __/__/____ Today I am Grateful For...

_____

_____

_____

_____

What Would Make Today A Great Day?

_____

_____

During the evening just before going to bed take a moment to reflect on your day then List

the 3 best things that happened...

1) _____

_____

2) _____

_____

3) _____

_____

Date: __/__/____ Today I am Grateful For...

_____

_____

_____

_____

What Would Make Today A Great Day?

_____

_____

During the evening just before going to bed take a moment to reflect on your day then List

the 3 best things that happened...

1) _____

_____

2) _____

_____

3) _____

_____

Date: __/__/____ Today I am Grateful For...

_____

_____

_____

_____

What Would Make Today A Great Day?

_____

_____

During the evening just before going to bed take a moment to reflect on your day then List

the 3 best things that happened...

1) _____

_____

2) _____

_____

3) _____

_____

Date: __/__/____ Today I am Grateful For...

_____

_____

_____

_____

What Would Make Today A Great Day?

_____

_____

During the evening just before going to bed take a moment to reflect on your day then

List the 3 best things that happened...

1) _____

_____

2) _____

_____

3) _____

_____

Date: __/__/____ Today I am Grateful For...

_____

_____

_____

_____

What Would Make Today A Great Day?

_____

_____

During the evening just before going to bed take a moment to reflect on your day then List the 3 best things that happened...

1) _____

_____

2) _____

_____

3) _____

_____

ABOUT THE AUTHOR

14-YEAR-OLD YASMINE BEN SALMI AKA LOVEPRENEUR

AS HEARD ON RADIO & AS SEEN ON TV & IN NEWSPAPERS & MAGAZINES

Purpose: To eradicate low self-esteem by liberating 1 million young people through the teaching of self-love

https://linktr.ee/YasmineBenSalmi

Guest speaker at Equinix "Global Happiness Speaker Series"

Yasmine is a Global Ambassador of IKAR Institute and representing of their #1MillionFutureLeaders Initiative: https://ikar.world/ikar-young-leaders/

Yasmine Ben Salmi aka LovePreneur is an 12yr old award-winning author of a book series called The Choice is Yours; The Choice is Yours - 10 Keys Principles to Create A Happier Lifestyle, The Choice is Yours – Your Thinking C.A.P for Living & Loving Life and The Choice is Yours – When I Chose To Be In The Choice.

Yasmine is a Podcast Host for a show called Life According To Yasmine:
https://yasminebensalmi.sounder.fm/show/a-letter-toyour-younger-self

The Ben Salmi d family were acknowledged during Chelsea FC - Edge of The Box 6th Anniversary celebration:
https://www.chelseafc.com/en/news/2021/12/15/edge-of-thebox-club-celebrates-six-year-anniversary

Brunel University London (B.U.L) have given the Ben Salmi family the opportunity to participate in Masterclasses covering Engineering, Computer Science and currently the Environmental Agency Masterclass.

Yasmine's youngest brother 8-year-old Amire is proud to be the youngest ever honorary STEM Ambassador in history for Brunel University London (B.U.L).

B.U.L has given the homeschooled families the opportunity to participate in masterclasses for the first time in history thanks to Lesley Warren.

Yasmine held her family's signature 2 Day Family workshop called Dreaming Big Together - Mamas Secret Recipe at The Hub Chelsea FC & Virgin Money.

Yasmine is the founder of The Choice Is Yours Publishing House.

Yasmine hosts her signature program called The Choice Is Yours - Your Thinking C.A.P For Living & Loving Life at Virgin Money Lounge

Yasmine participated in campaigns for Sainsburys, Legoland, Warner Bros, Sony and Made for Mums to name a few.

Yasmine's signature program: Your Thinking C.A.P for Living & Loving Life™

Yasmine is the founder of Dog Walking Service "Woof-Woof your dog is here".

Yasmine was nominated for a R.E.E.B.A Award 2017, Winner of Radio Works Authors Awards 2017 and nominated for National Diversity Award 2017.

Yasmine was invited to be a guest speaker at The Best You Expo: https://youtu.be/Fz9mErJC8rA where there were 15,000 attendees and a former International Radio Show Host

Yasmine is also the founder of Mother and Daughter Connect Collection and founder of Lovepreneur.

Yasmine dreams to be the change that she desires to see in the world and inspire others to be in the choice as often as possible.

The question is when will you start living life on your terms?

Book:

(1) The Choice Is Yours: Your Thinking C.A.P for Living &
Loving Life part 2
https://www.amazon.co.uk/dp/1913310167/ref=cm_sw_r_
cp_api_i_yanEEbMNHWH6M

(2) The Choice Is Yours: When I Chose To Be in The Choice
https://www.amazon.co.uk/dp/B08946D6Y9/ref=cm_sw_r
_cp_api_i_GJk1Eb72EDZ5V

(3) My First Day: Transitioning from Girlhood To Womanhood
https://www.amazon.co.uk/dp/1913310299/ref=cm_sw_r_
em_api_fabc_GGYGMR20HDYS7XNH2DPB

(4) THE CHOICE IS YOURS: I'm Not Just A Pretty F.A.C.E - I
AM Intelligent Too: 4
https://www.amazon.co.uk/dp/1913310566/ref=cm_sw_r_
cp_api_glt_fabc_VDGJ8MC7X7RE6RJV8HNY
(5)

Facebook page:

Lovepreneure:
https://m.facebook.com/YasmineBenSalmiakaLovePrenur/

BEN SALMI FAMILY MANTRA

"BEN SALMI TEAMWORK MAKES THE DREAMWORK

We believe that there is no such thing as failure, only feedback.

We also believe that the journey of one thousand miles begins with a single step in the right direction

FAMILY ANTHEM

If you want to be somebody,
If you want to go somewhere, You better
wake up and **PAY ATTENTION!**

I'm ready to be somebody,
I'm ready to go somewhere, I'm ready to
wake up and **PAY ATTENTION!**

The question is ARE **YOU**?

MEET THE DOCTOR

Chidiebere Ibe, BSc is the only Nigerian Medical Illustrator and a professional among the few in Africa. He is the Creative Director at the Association of Future African Neurosurgeons (AFAN), Young Continental Association of African Neurosurgical Societies (YCAANS) and Creative Director and Chief Medical Illustrator of the Journal of Global Neurosurgery. He is also a Junior Committee Member-World Federation of Neurosurgeons - Global Neurosurgery. Chidiebere Ibe is passionate about contemporary illustrations of black patients. He has worked assiduously to promote the use of black skin medical illustration in medical textbooks and public health materials, this has afforded him the opportunity to be featured in WebMD/Medscape, Maryland

Neurosurgery and Global Scalpels podcast and other reputable institutions globally. He hopes to pursue a career in paediatric neurosurgery and establish an association for black illustrators.

If you would like to follow Chidiebere on his journey to become a Neurosurgeon follow his social media:

LinkedIn:
https://www.linkedin.com/mwlite/in/chidiebere-ibe-206ab81a9

Instagram:
https://www.instagram.com/ebereillustrate/?hl=en

Facebook:
https://m.facebook.com/Chidiesquire1?tsid=0.2492054895007002 &source=result

You can also check out his interview with NBC Washington News4.

https://www.nbcwashington.com/news/health/students-medicalillustrat ions-showing-black-people-go-viral/2904140/

Check out Mr Chidiebere Ibe amazing illustrations, you can find even more on his social media.

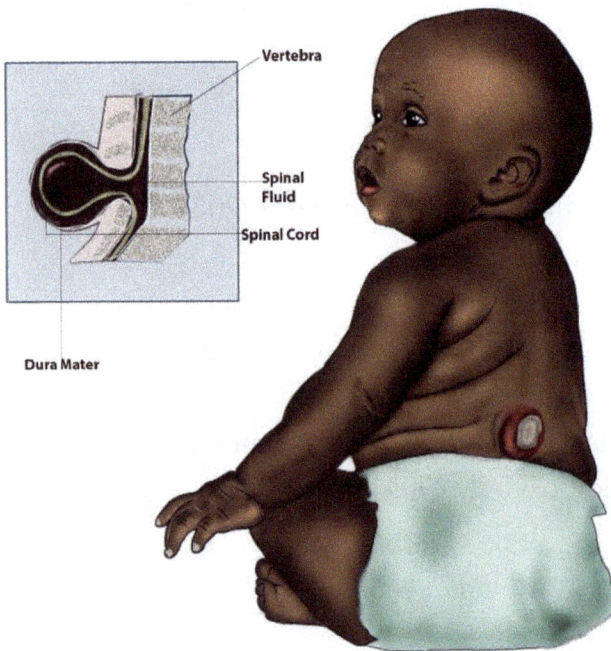

Vertebra

Spinal Fluid

Spinal Cord

Dura Mater

SPINA BIFIDA

Spina bifida is a birth defect that occurs when the spine and spinal cord don't form properly.
It's a type of neural tube defect.
There are three main types:
spina bifida occulta, meningocele and myelomeningocele.

Chidiebere Ibe
IG: ebereillustrate
Twitter: ebereillustrate

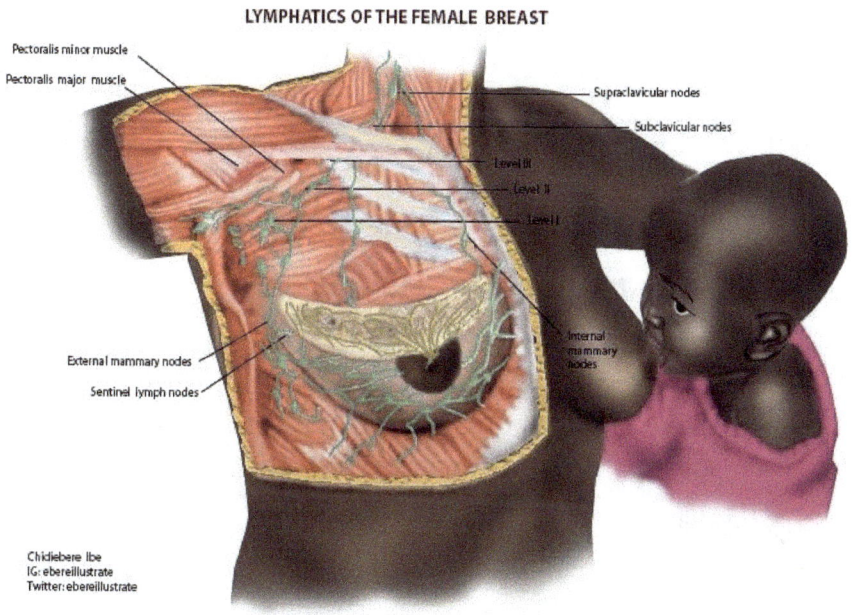

LYMPHATICS OF THE FEMALE BREAST

Pectoralis minor muscle

Pectoralis major muscle

Supraclavicular nodes

Subclavicular nodes

Level III

Level II

Level I

Internal mammary nodes

External mammary nodes

Sentinel lymph nodes

Chidiebere Ibe
IG: ebereillustrate
Twitter: ebereillustrate

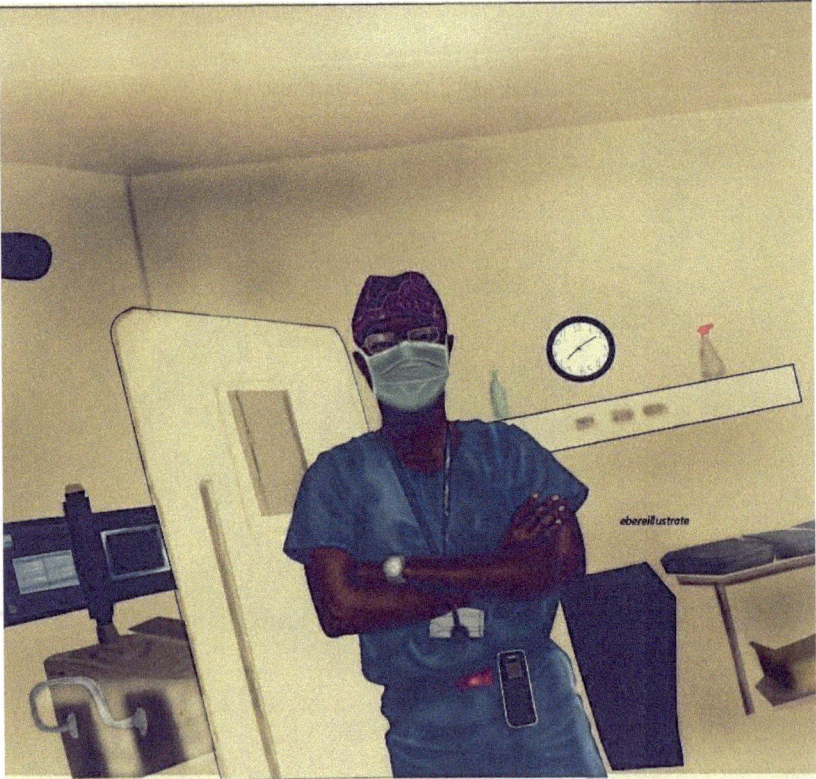

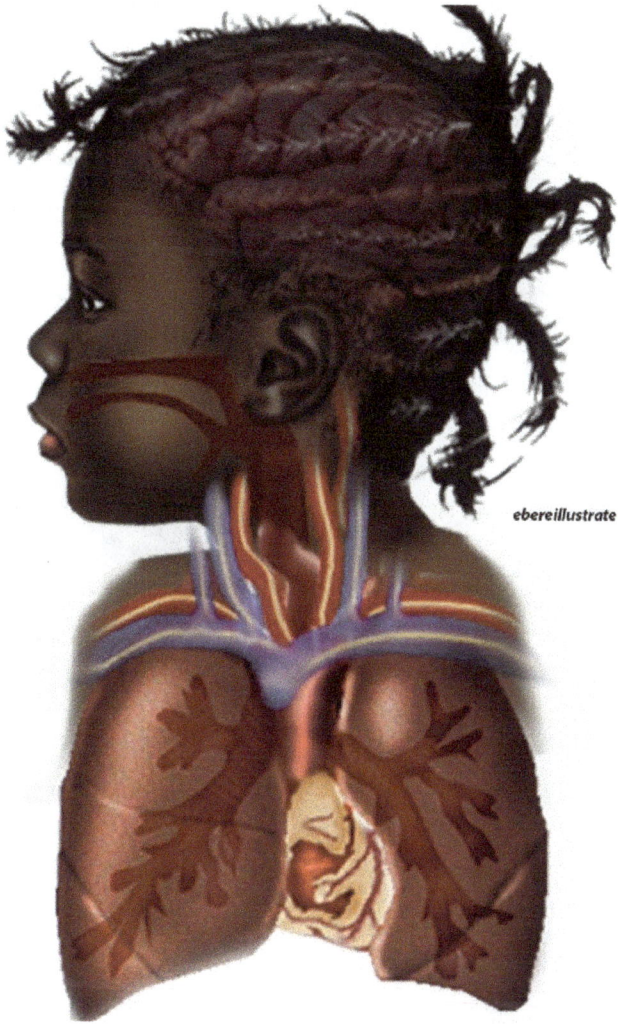

ebereillustrate

OVARIAN CANCER

Ovarian cancer is a type of cancer that begins in the ovaries.
Ovarian cancer often goes undetected until it has spread within the pelvis and abdomen.
At this late stage, ovarian cancer is more difficult to treat.
Early-stage ovarian cancer, in which the disease is confined to the ovary,
is more likely to be treated successfully.

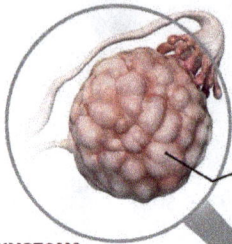

Cancerous ovary

SYMPTOMS

Early-stage ovarian cancer rarely
causes any symptoms.

Abdominal bloating or swelling

Quickly feeling full when eating

Weight loss

Discomfort in the pelvis area

A frequent need to urinate

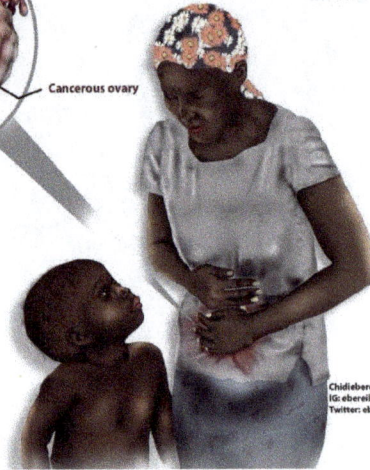

Chidiebere Ibe
IG: ebereillustrate
Twitter: ebereillustrate

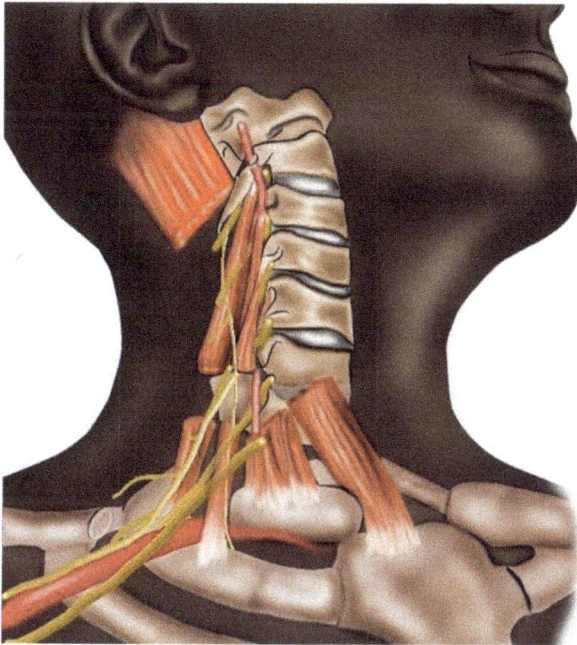

**ANATOMICAL
ILLUSTRATION**

Chidiebere Ibe
IG: ebereillustrate
Twitter:ebereillustrate